Fish addition

Start on 3. Hop on 2. Land on 5. $3 + 2 = 5$

Start on 2. Hop on 3. Land on 5. $2 + 3 = 5$

$1 + 5 = \square$

$5 + 1 = \square$

$4 + 4 = \square$

$4 + 4 = \square$

$3 + 4 = \square$

$4 + 3 = \square$

$6 + 3 = \square$

$3 + 6 = \square$

$5 + 3 = \square$

$3 + 5 = \square$

$8 + 1 = \square$

$1 + 8 = \square$

$6 + 4 = \square$

$4 + 6 = \square$

$9 + 1 = \square$

$1 + 9 = \square$

$8 + 0 = \square$

$0 + 8 = \square$

$3 + 7 = \square$

$7 + 3 = \square$

$2 + 8 = \square$

$8 + 2 = \square$

$7 + 2 = \square$

$2 + 7 = \square$

Does it matter which number comes first when you add two numbers together?

Date

Sort the beads

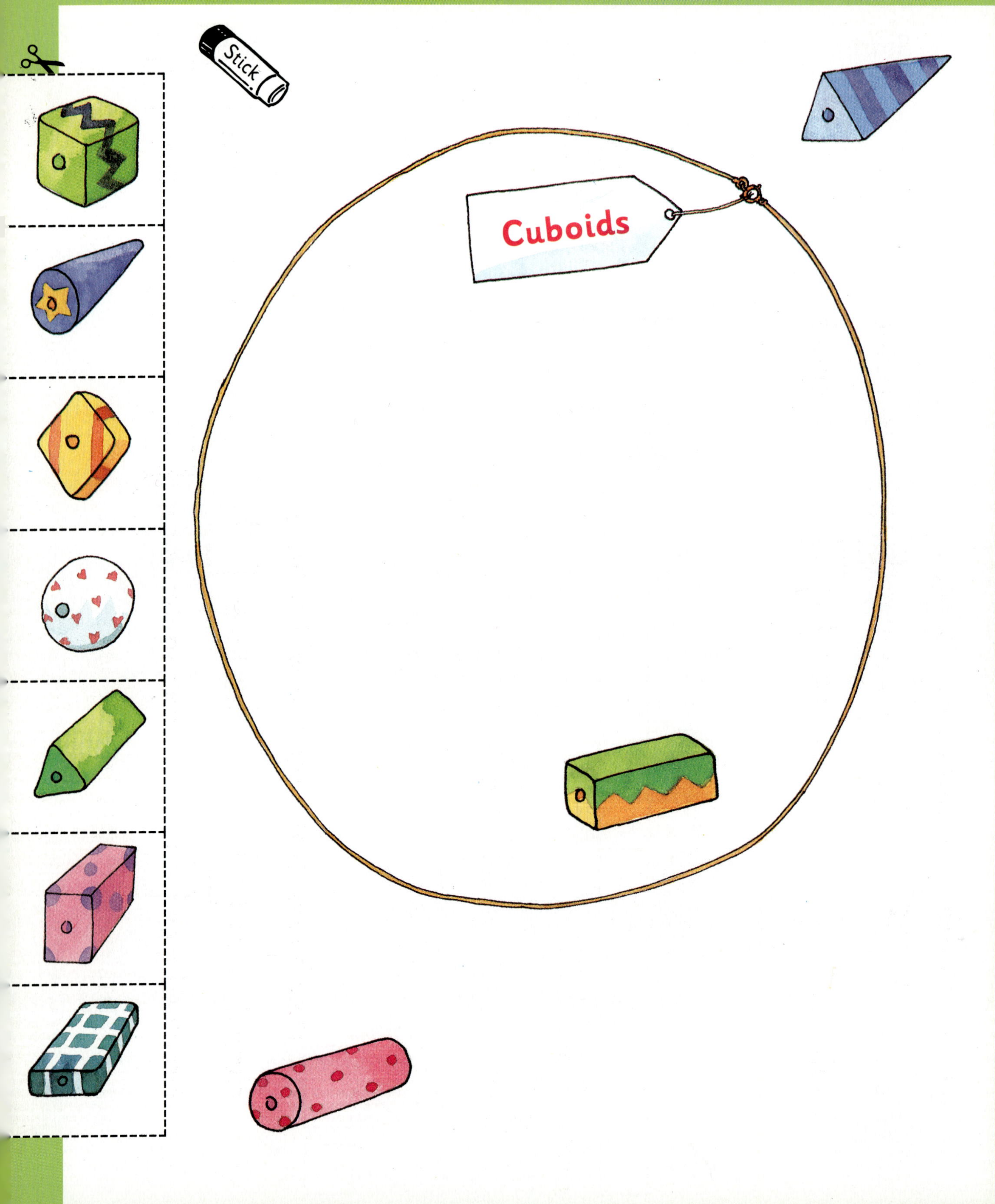

What other ways could you sort these shapes?

Date

2:2 3-D shape (1)
Sorting and naming 3-D shapes.

EXTRA STEPS MATHEMATICS

2a

Name

Hop addition

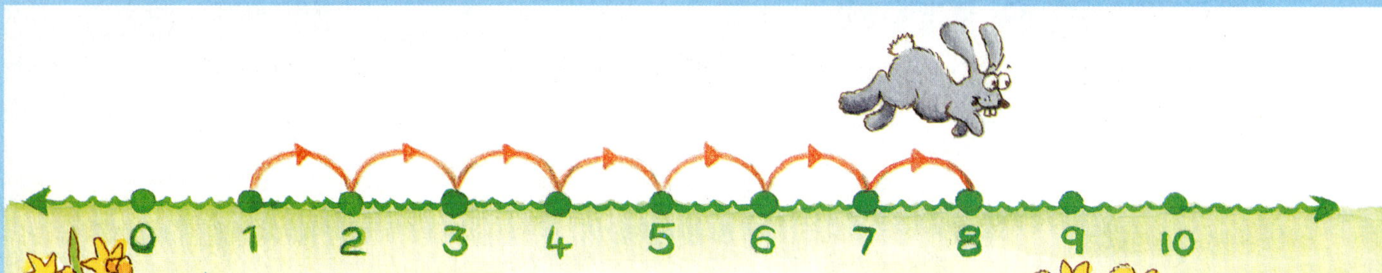

1 + 7 = 8

1 + 4 = ☐

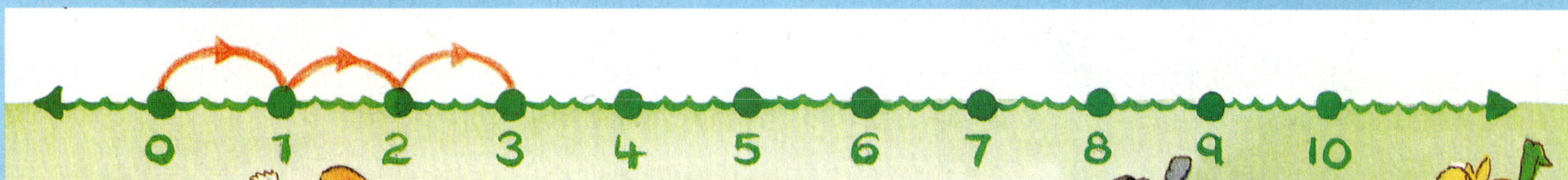

0 + ☐ = ☐

☐ + ☐ = ☐

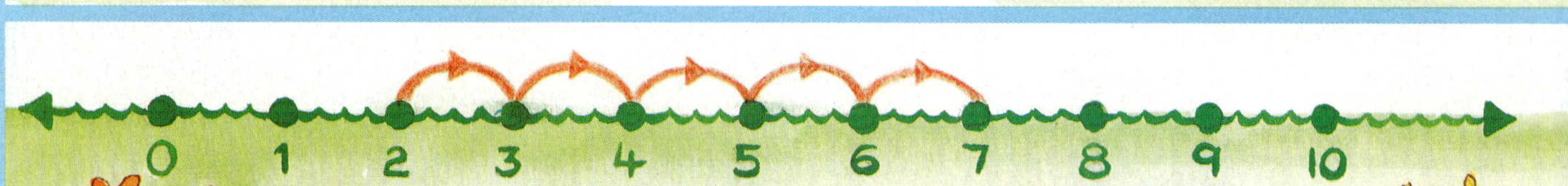

☐ + ☐ = ☐

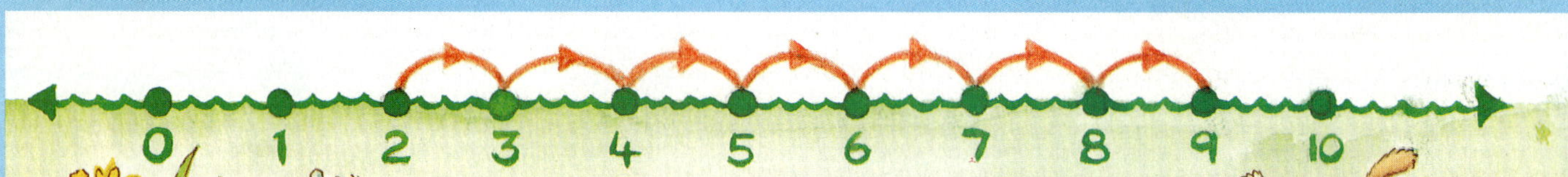

☐ + ☐ = ☐

Can you make up some more?

Date

2:1 Addition 0 – 10
Using a number line to 'count on'.

Croc-shapes

How many of these shapes can you see:

- prisms ☐
- spheres ☐
- pyramids ☐
- cuboids ☐
- cylinders ☐
- cones ☐

Count the shapes in the picture which have:

- curved faces ☐
- circular faces ☐
- flat faces ☐
- triangular faces ☐
- square faces ☐
- oblong faces ☐

You can use 3-D shapes to help you.

What else can you tell me about this animal?

Date

2:2 3-D shape (1)
Using and interpreting shape vocabulary.

Hop subtraction

Start on 8. Hop back 2. Land on 6.

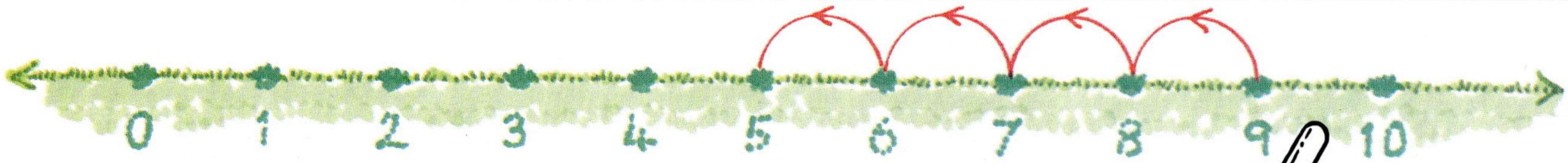

Start on 9. Hop back 4. Land on ☐.

Start on 10. Hop back ☐. Land on ☐.

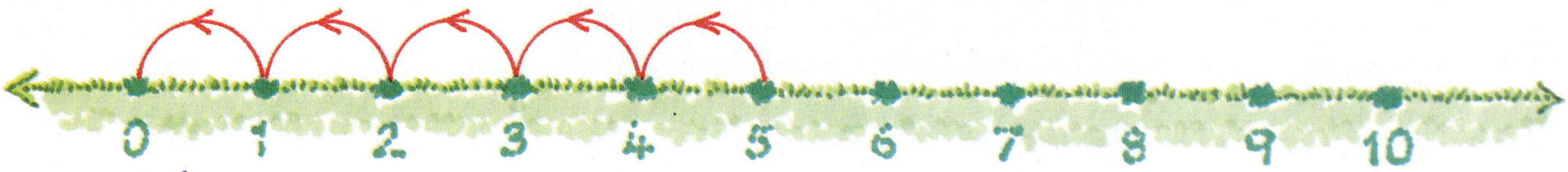

Start on ☐. Hop back ☐. Land on ☐.

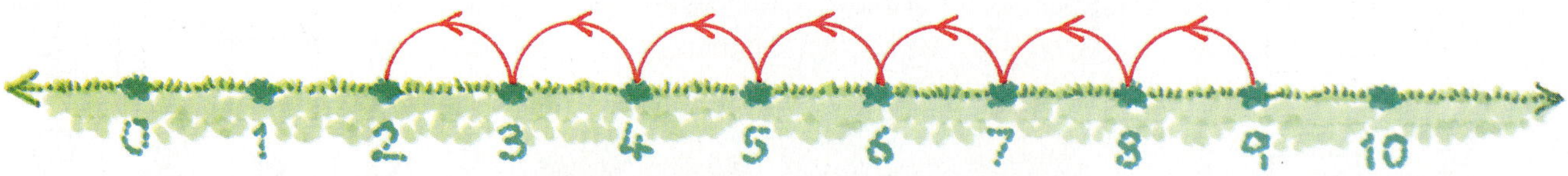

Start on ☐. Hop back ☐. Land on ☐.

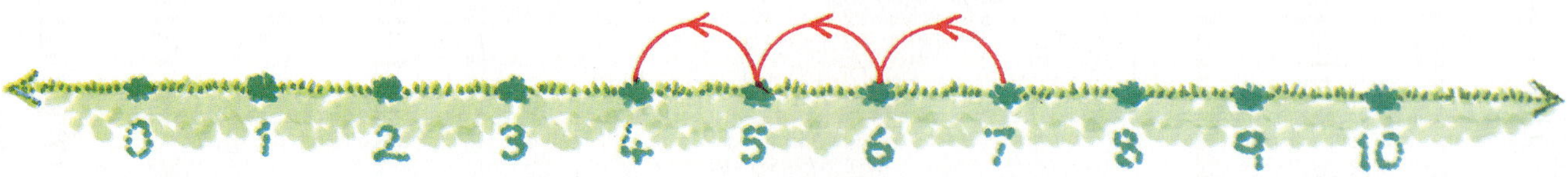

Start on ☐. Hop back ☐. Land on ☐.

Can you make up some more?

Date

Counting back

Start on 7. Hop back 2. Land on 5. 7 – 2 = 5

9 – 8 = ☐

1 – 1 = ☐

10   5 = ☐

8 – 3 = ☐

7 – 4 = ☐

4 – 1 = ☐

6 – 3 = ☐

6 – 2 = ☐

5 – 4 = ☐

9 – 6 = ☐

3 – 1 = ☐

2 – 1 = ☐

10 – 7 = ☐

8 – 6 = ☐

Date

Reflections

Complete the reflections. You can use a mirror to help you.

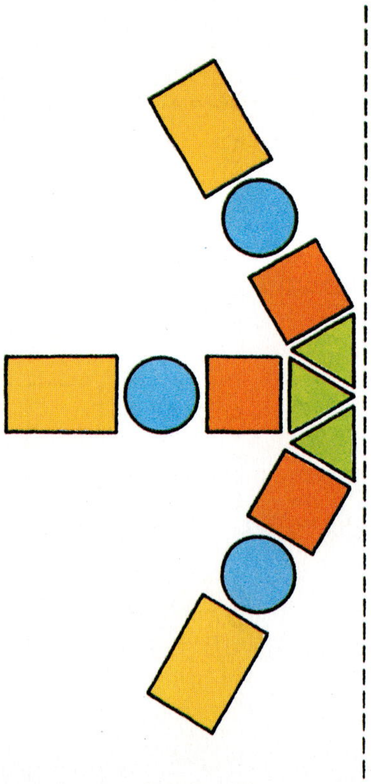

This pattern can have 2 mirror lines.
Draw the missing line then colour.

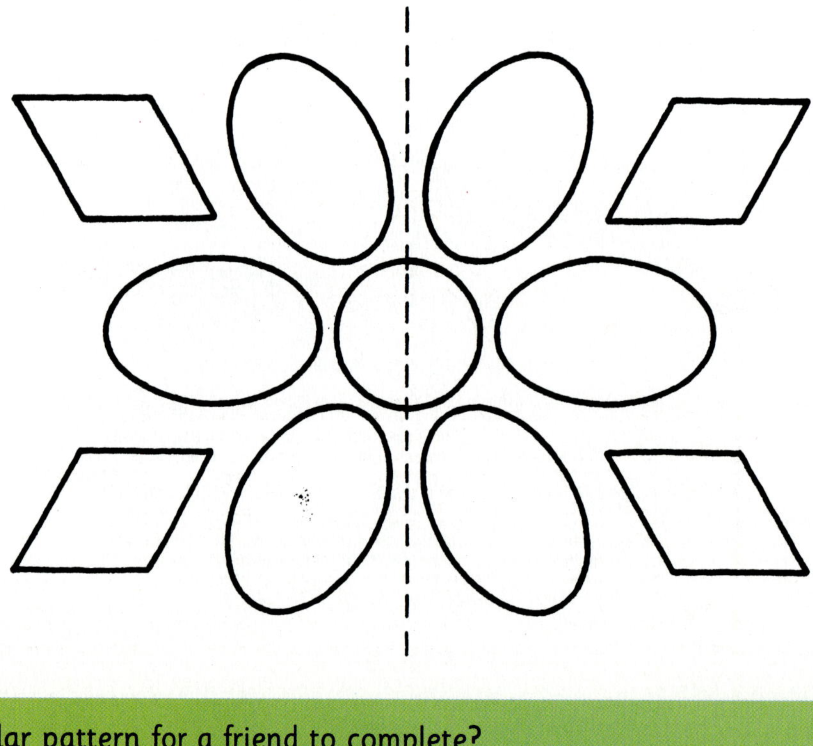

Can you draw a similar pattern for a friend to complete?

Date

2:4 Reflection
Completing patterns which have line symmetry.

Missing numbers

3 + 4 = □

1 + 9 = □

2 + 7 = □

8 + 1 = □

6 + 4 = □

3 + 2 = □

5 + 5 = □

4 + 4 = □

4 + ○ = □

7 + ○ = □

3 + ○ = □

5 + ○ = □

2 + ○ = □

1 + ○ = □

6 + ○ = □

4 + ○ = □

△ + ○ = 9

△ + ○ = 2

△ + ○ = 1

△ + ○ = 6

△ + ○ = 3

△ + ○ = 8

△ + ○ = 7

△ + ○ = 5

△ + ○ = 4

△ + ○ = 10

How many other ways can you find to make ten?

Date

2:5 Addition patterns to 10
Understanding the use of a symbol to stand for an unknown number.

Patterns of 9

Complete.

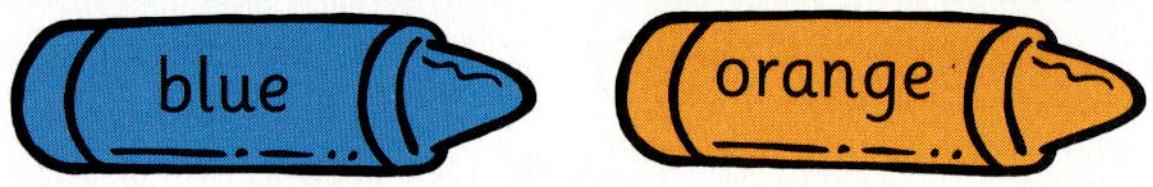

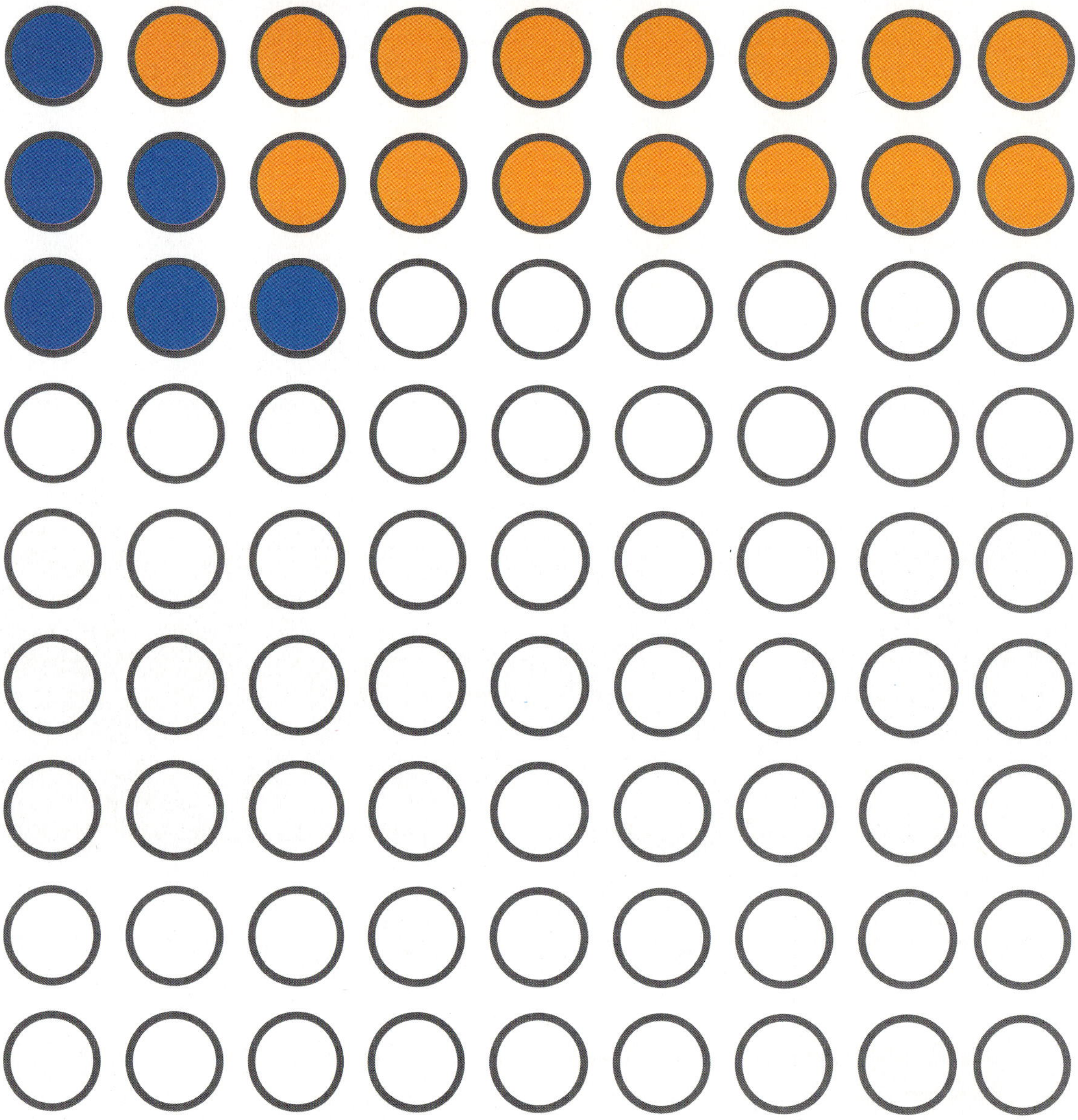

1 + 8 = 9　　　( ) + ( ) = ( )　　　( ) + ( ) = ( )

2 + 7 = ( )　　　( ) + ( ) = ( )　　　( ) + ( ) = ( )

3 + ( ) = ( )　　　( ) + ( ) = ( )　　　( ) + ( ) = ( )

Can you find number patterns for eight?

Date

2:5 Addition patterns to 10
Finding pairs of numbers which total 9.

Dogs and owners

Join each owner to a dog to make 7 each time.

7 + 0 = 7

6 + ☐ = 7

☐ + ☐ = 7

☐ + ☐ = 7

☐ + ☐ = 7

☐ + ☐ = 7

☐ + ☐ = 7

☐ + ☐ = 7

Date

2:5 Addition patterns to 10
Finding pairs of numbers which total 7.

Finding subtraction patterns

8

8 − 0 = ○
8 − 3 = ○
8 − 8 = ○
8 − 6 = ○
8 − 1 = ○
8 − 5 = ○
8 − 2 = ○
8 − 7 = ○
8 − 4 = ○

7

7 − 3 = ○
7 − 6 = ○
7 − 2 = ○
7 − 4 = ○
7 − 1 = ○
7 − 7 = ○
7 − 5 = ○
7 − 0 = ○

8 − 0 = ○
8 − 1 = ○
□ − □ = ○
□ − □ = ○
□ − □ = ○
□ − □ = ○
□ − □ = ○
□ − □ = ○
□ − □ = ○

7 − 0 = ○
7 − 1 = ○
□ − □ = ○
□ − □ = ○
□ − □ = ○
□ − □ = ○
□ − □ = ○
□ − □ = ○

Find subtraction patterns for other numbers.

Date

2:6 Subtraction patterns to 10
Exploring patterns in subtraction.

Balancing the sums

6 + 4 = 10

7 + 3 = 10

9 + ☐ = 10

2 + ☐ = 10

5 + ☐ = 10

8 + ☐ = 10

☐ + 7 = 10

1 + ☐ = 10

☐ + 6 = 10

8 + ☐ = 9

2 + ☐ = 5

1 + ☐ = 3

4 + ☐ = 6

6 + ☐ = 7

☐ + 1 = 4

1 + ☐ = 2

☐ + 3 = 8

Date

Boot sale bargains

The difference in price is ☐ p.

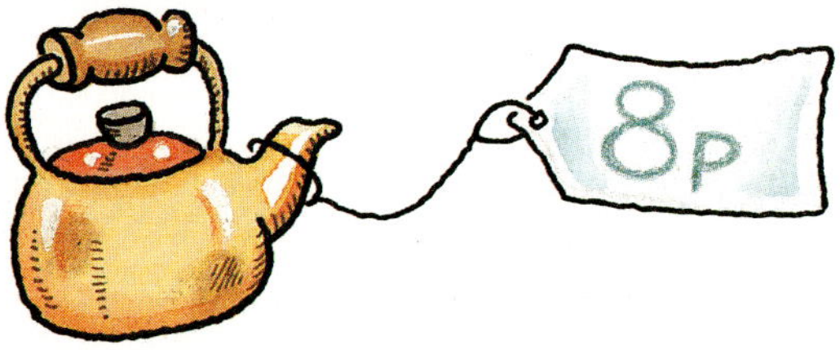

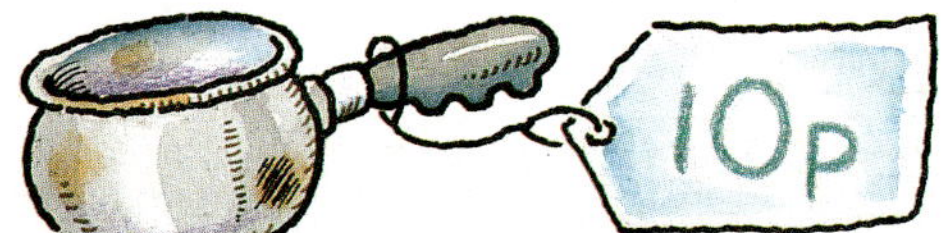

The difference in price is ☐ p.

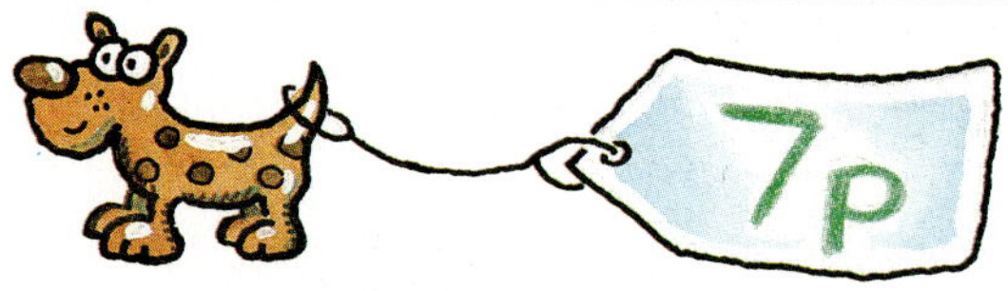

The difference in price is ☐ p.

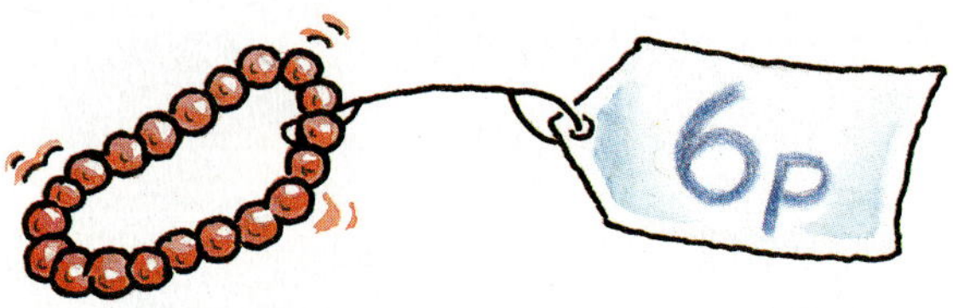

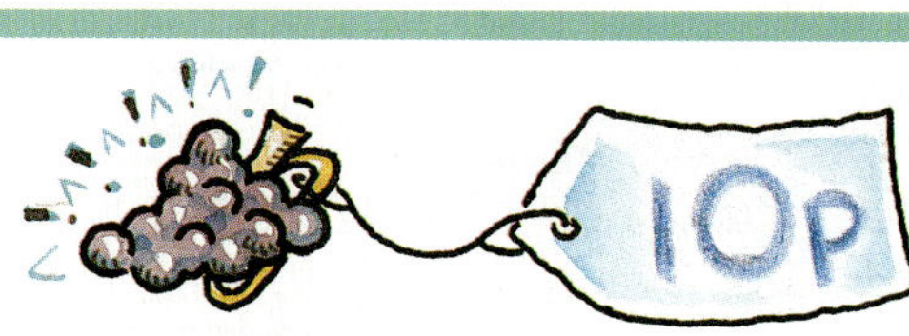

The difference in price is ☐ p.

The difference in price is ☐ p.

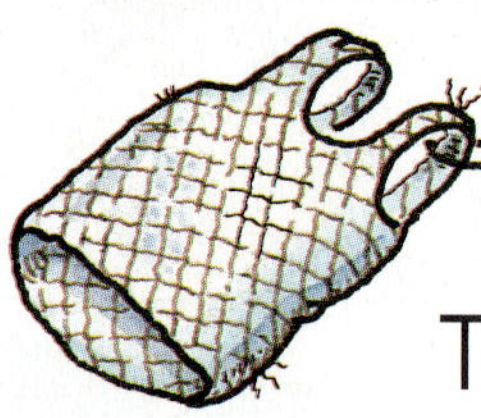

The difference in price is ☐ p.

The difference in price is ☐ p.

 Date

2:6 Subtraction patterns to 10
Comparing 2 numbers to find the difference.

Grouping in tens

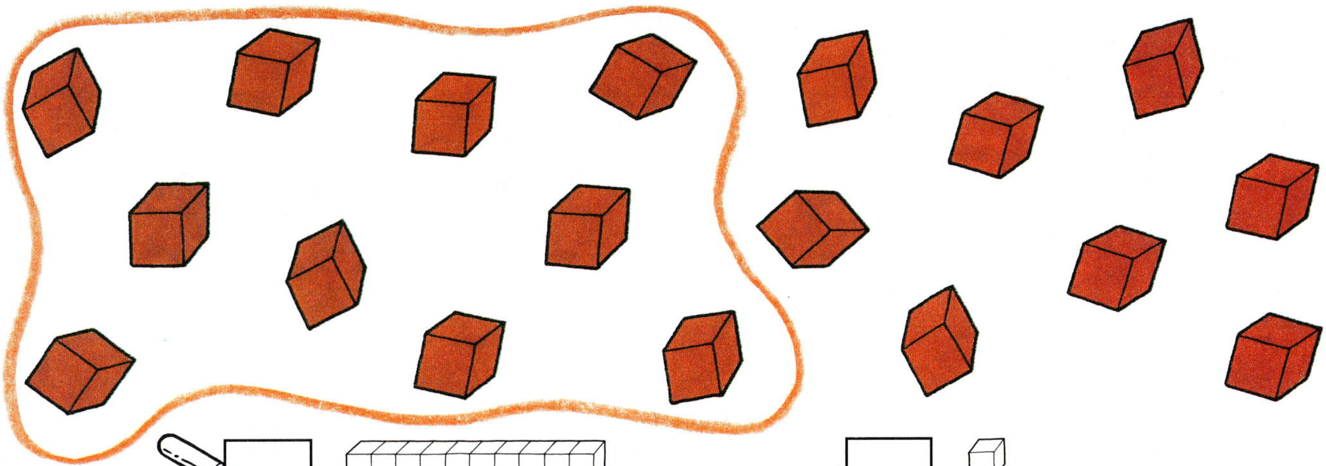

☐ longs ☐ ones

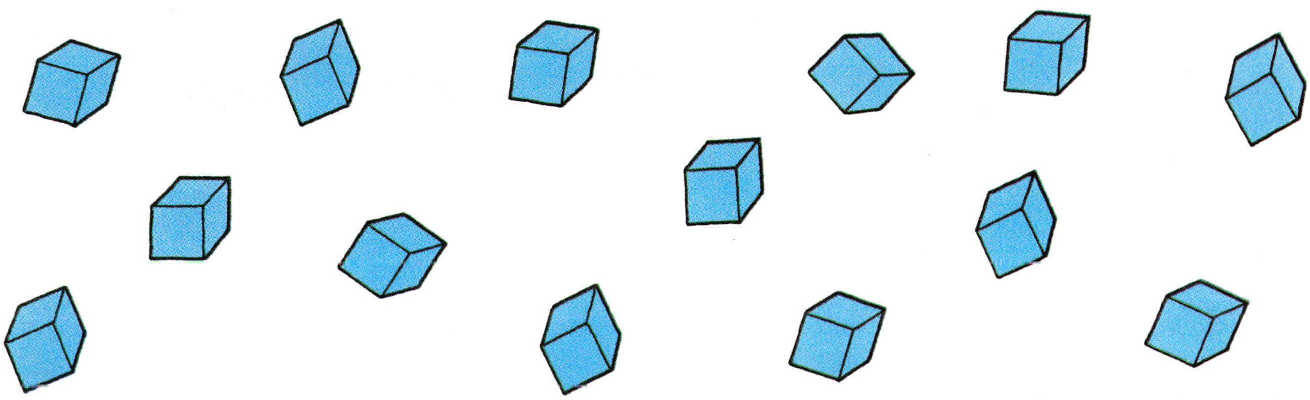

☐ longs ☐ ones

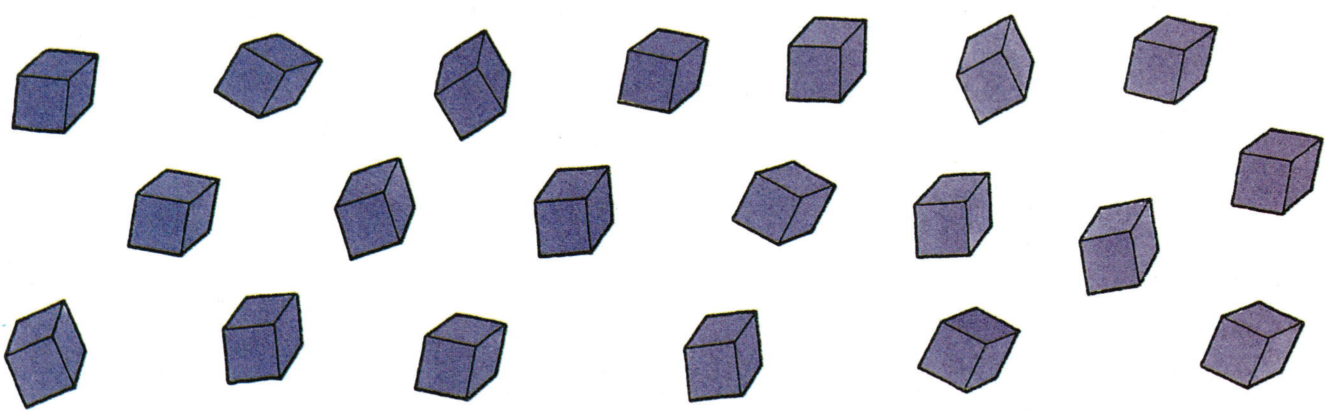

☐ longs ☐ ones

Can you design a cube-grouping sheet for a friend?

Date

2:7 Place value
Representing grouping in tens.

Loop the groups

☐ groups of 5 ☐ ones

☐ groups of 8 ☐ ones

 Date

☐ groups of 6 ☐ ones

☐ groups of 9 ☐ ones

Can you design a picture to show groups of seven?

2:7 Place value (1)
Representing numbers up to 20 as groups and ones.

Patchwork quilt

Colour.

oblongs
hexagons
squares
circles
triangles
pentagons

What other shapes can you see in the room?

Date

2:8 2-D shape (1)
Recognising names of 2-D shapes.

Dot-to-dot

Can you make a dot-to-dot picture for a friend?

Date

2:9 Counting to 20
Counting and writing numbers to 20.

Estimating and counting

Estimate first, then count.

estimated

counted

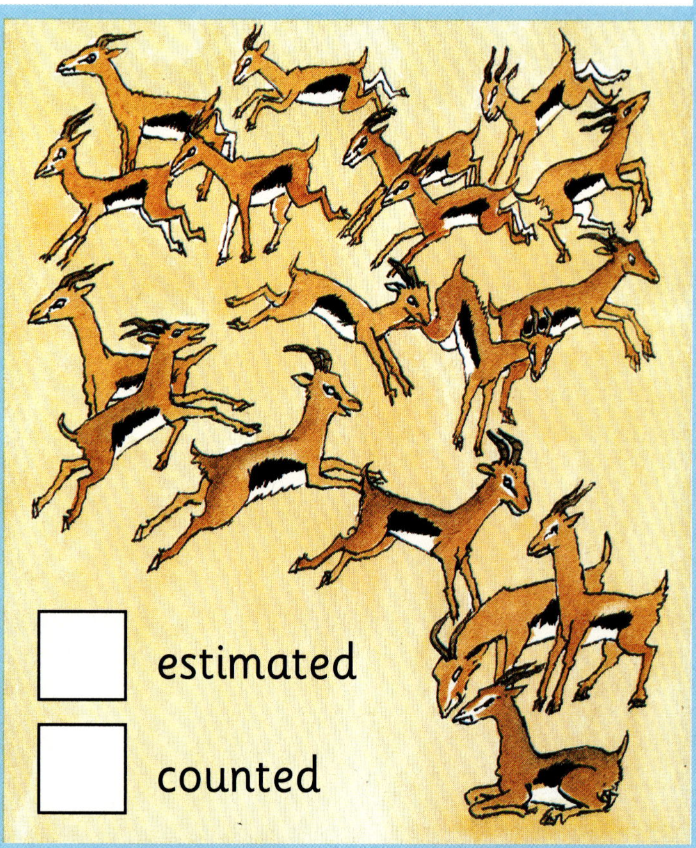

estimated

counted

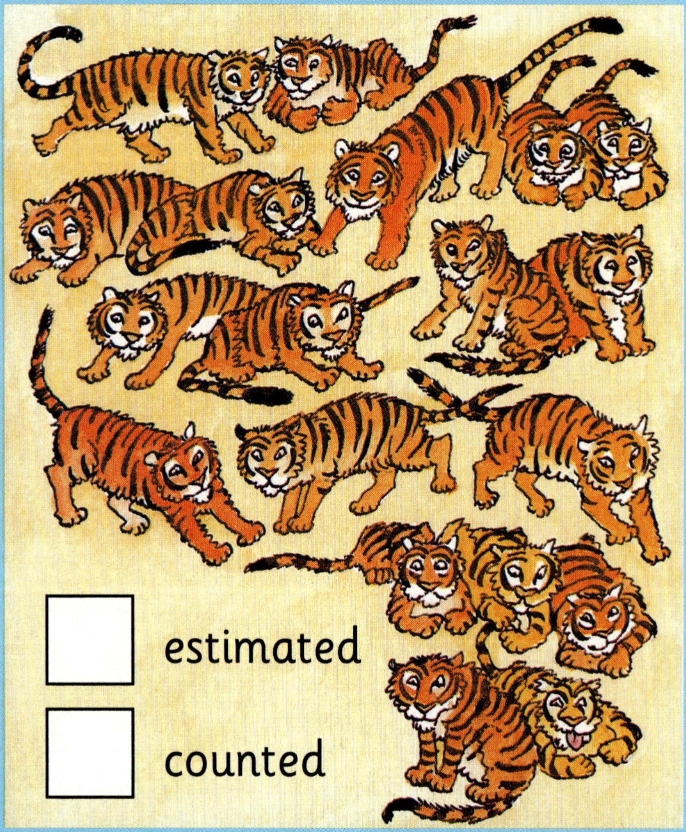

estimated

counted

estimated

counted

Which animal are there the most of?

Date

Juggling sets

Draw the right number of shapes in each hoop.

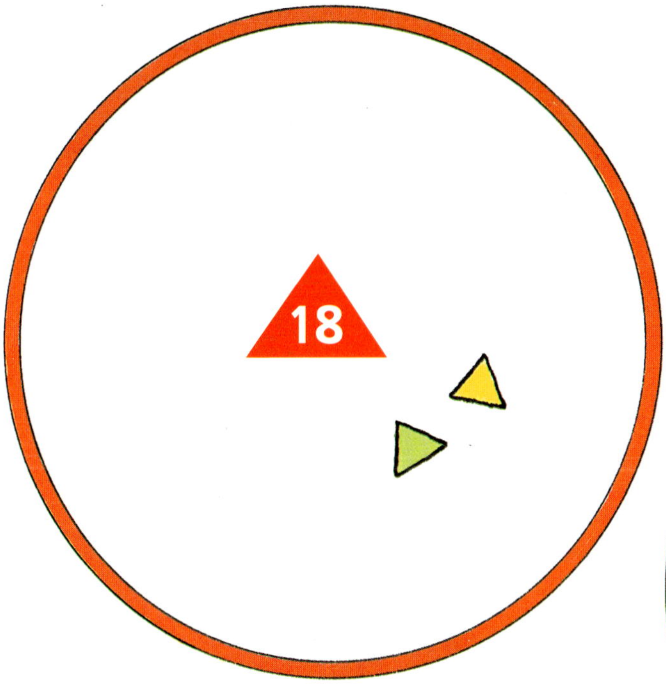

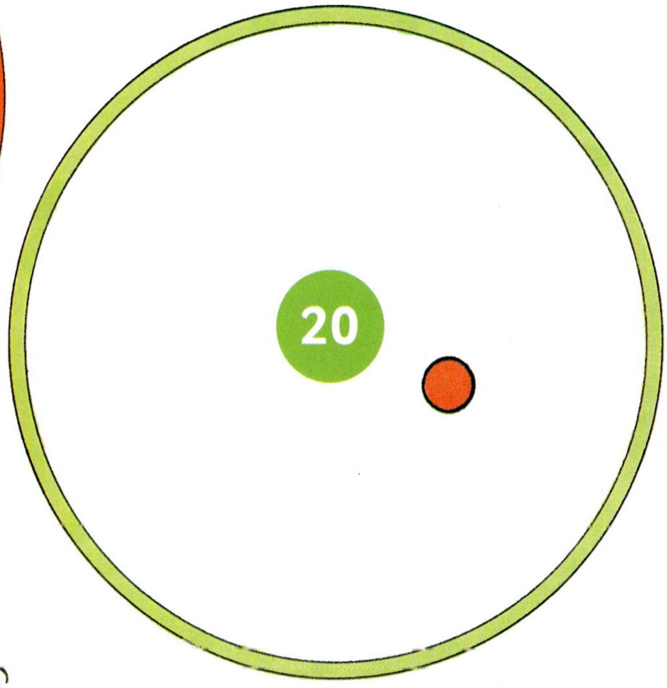

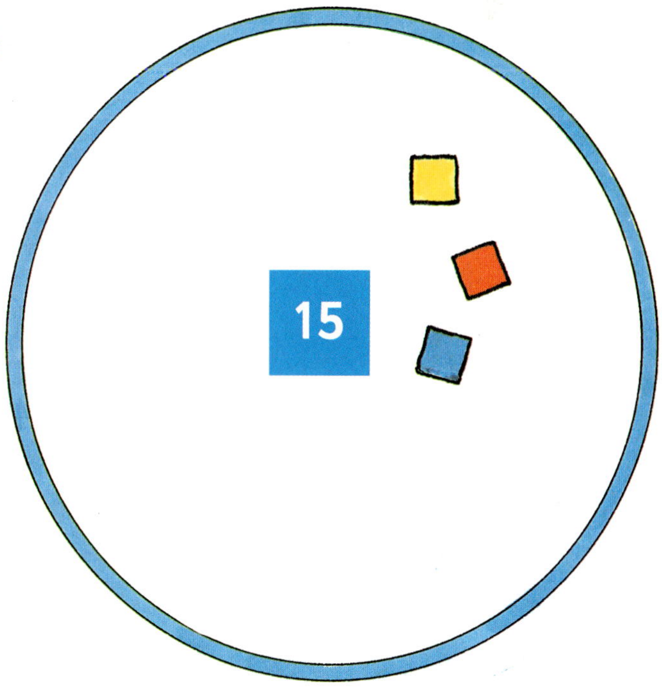

Date

Garden path

Jane and her grandad measured the length of their garden path.

Estimate how long the path is in Grandad's and then Jane's foot lengths.

Now count.

	estimate	count
Grandad's foot lengths		
Jane's foot lengths		

Jane used ☐ more foot lengths than Grandad. Why?

What do you think would happen if Jane's mum measured the path with **her** foot length?

Date

2:10 Length (1)
Measuring using non-standard units.

Night sky numbers

Under the sea

Date

Which creature are there the most of?

2:11 Place value (2)
Understanding the composition of numbers up to 20 as 'tens and ones'.

Carpet areas

Which is the biggest carpet? Does it have the most shapes?

Date

2:12 Area
Counting shapes to find area.

Snake sums

Use numbers from 1 to 9 to make these totals.

[5] + [2] + [4] = 11

[ ] + [ ] + [ ] = 12

[ ] + [ ] + [ ] = 13

[ ] + [ ] + [ ] = 14

[ ] + [ ] + [ ] = 15

[ ] + [ ] + [ ] = 16

[ ] + [ ] + [ ] = 17

[ ] + [ ] + [ ] = 18

[ ] + [ ] + [ ] = 19

[ ] + [ ] + [ ] = 20

Shade the totals on the snake the right colour.

Date

Marvellous money-box

or

Put in different combinations of coins. Can you take out an odd amount?

 Date

Twenty search

Loop pairs of numbers which make 20.

Can you see a hidden letter?

Can you make a scroll for a friend with number pairs that make 19?

Date

Honeycomb addition

Make each side total 20. You can use counters to help you.

Make each side total 15.

Magic pattern

1 + 10 = ☐	6 + 10 = ☐
2 + 10 = ☐	7 + 10 = ☐
3 + 10 = ☐	8 + 10 = ☐
4 + 10 = ☐	9 + 10 = ☐
5 + 10 = ☐	10 + 10 = ☐

Complete and colour the patterns.

7, 8, 9, ☐, 11, 12, ☐, ☐, ☐

1, 3, ☐, 7, 9, ☐, ☐, ☐, ☐

0, ☐, 6, 9, ☐, ☐, 18

2, 4, ☐, ☐, 10, ☐, ☐, ☐, ☐

5, 8, ☐, ☐, ☐, 17, ☐

Date

EXTRA STEPS Book 2a

This book is part of the STEPS MATHEMATICS scheme

Published 1994 by
Collins Educational (an imprint of HarperCollins*Publishers*)
77-85 Fulham Palace Road
Hammersmith
London W6 8JB

ISBN 0 00 312633-1

Series Editor:
Anne Woodman

Author:
Margaret Williams

Cover illustration:
Wendy Sinclair

Illustrations:
Olivia Bown
Juliet Breese
Mike Levy
Jenny Mumford
Archie Plumb
Wendy Sinclair
Martin Ursell

Design and setting:
The Design Works, Reading

Printed and bound by:
Stige-Arti Grafiche,
Italy

ISBN 0-00-312633-1
9 780003 126334 >

Saria

Anna

Thomas

Owen

Buying fruit

Saria, Thomas, Anna and Owen were each given 10p to spend at the fruit stall.

The pictures above show the fruit they bought.

Look at the prices on the front cover.

How much money does each child have left?
What fruit can they each buy with the money they have left?

Collins Educational